PROTOCOLS AN ERASURE

Daniela Naomi Molnar

"'We are repeat children,' poet Daniela Naomi Molnar writes in this searing, necessary meditation on inherited trauma, cycles of violence, and the possibility of healing. *PROTOCOLS: An Erasure* is a fragmented psalm, an outcry, a fractured cultural memoir, and a gripping and timely reflection on how we human beings can choose to use language to destroy—or to rebuild."
—**Alicia Jo Rabins**, author of *Fruit Geode* and *Divinity School*

"This book is oracular, tender, and absolutely brilliant. Daniela Naomi Molnar looked into a foundational antisemitic text and traced a radiant meditation on power and being. Her essay about her grandmother Rosalie contains some of the best writing I have read about ancestry, inheritance, and survival. This book is a blessing, a transmutation of suffering into a spacious body of language and light."
—**Rachel Jamison Webster**, author of *Benjamin Banneker and Us*

"*PROTOCOLS: An Erasure* is a text that holds within it the complexity of inherited Jewish trauma, the courage to reject exceptionalism and its supremacist logics, and the tenderness to honor loss and cradle the grieving body across generations. In *PROTOCOLS: An Erasure,* Daniela Naomi Molnar asks: 'How to not be history's accomplice?' This book is a master class on grief and the creative, regenerative impulse, metabolizing trauma and loss into a form that both mourns and resists. Brave, meticulous, haunting, and brilliant, this book was a journey of transfiguration, a widening of my mind."
—**Mónica Gomery**, author of *Might Kindred*

"At once a reckoning and a declaration, Daniela Naomi Molnar demands of the past a yielding to something new. Leaving traces of historical violence visible while aspiring to 'that / which cannot be / individual,' Molnar carves through the pages of histories' hauntings to sculpt a new surface, textured with liberatory possibilities, laced with the temptations and catastrophes of belonging, and reaching towards care—towards 'a new, spacious body through which to speak.'"
—**Rachel Kaufman**, author of *Many to Remember*

"In her unflinching work *PROTOCOLS: An Erasure*, Daniela Naomi Molnar reexamines one of the most antisemitic documents in world history, asking us 'to return to the / center / to be / nothing / honestly.' Molnar's brilliant erasure reveals her generous, undaunted craft, inventing new sites of possibility that emerge—even from the abhorrent ruins of the source text. Molnar lyrically asserts that, even amid despair and cynicism, 'our hands   exist / as love,   a boundless / agriculture / of intelligence.'"
—**Rosebud Ben-Oni**, author of *If This Is the Age We End Discovery*

Ayin books are made possible through the generous support of the Opaline Fund, Anne Germanacos, and Lippman Kanfer Foundation for Living Torah. We are grateful for their commitment to the transformative power of creative work, and to amplifying a polyphony of voices from within and beyond the Jewish world.

The author also gratefully acknowledges Regional Arts & Culture Council for essential support of her work on *PROTOCOLS: An Erasure*.

Regional Arts & Culture Council

Cover design by Rebecca Leffell Koren
Book design and typesetting by Rebecca Leffell Koren

Typeset in Adobe Kis VF, designed by Robert Slimbach, released by Adobe Originals; Century Oldstyle STD, designed by Morris Fuller Benton, released by American Type Founders in 1909 and licensed by Adobe; and American Typewriter, designed by Joel Kaden and Tony Stan, released by International Typeface Corporation in 1974 and licensed by Adobe.

First Edition
First Printing

Ayin Press
Brooklyn, New York
www.ayinpress.org
info@ayinpress.org

Distributed by Publishers Group West, an Ingram brand
Printed in the USA

ISBN (paperback): 978-1-961814-23-3
ISBN (e-book): 978-1-961814-24-0

Library of Congress Control Number: 2024949066

PROTOCOLS: AN ERASURE / MINUTES: A REMEMBRANCE

this material is responsible for

Theft, mutilation

and dismissal from

Center

QVOD SVPERIVS MACROPROSOPVS
QVOD INFERIVS

(Eliphas Levi)

the Serpent

has been

the

only one

to let waters remain still

to return to the

center

to be

nothing

honestly

apparently

the bearer of

a whole

mind

may observe

the whole world.

Beware!

the inevitable

ordinary

truths

root

and flow

omit

power and

authority

embroider

instead

with

trust

with mass

to secure

life's

magnificent

swivel

PROTOCOL 1

instincts
are obtained by

(power)

sacrificing

order

and blind
force to

freedom

(power)

(power)

(power)

(power)

gold

flames make

(power)

internal

life

and hope

governs

possibility

both mysteries and

certainty

are guided by

nothing

(power)

(power)

(power)

visible

attention
is not

a

(the crowd)
(the crowd)

void

(the crowd) (the people)

(the mass)

(the people)

(the masses)

(power)

(the mass)

quiet

(the mass)

hands of

(the masses)

(the crowd)

(the mob)

animals

and

(the people)

women — their

sheer force

indispensable

(power)

(power)

(power)

(power)

(the people)

(the mob)

to Nature

(the mob)   (power)

ecstasy

and peace

gave us
ourselves

we

hand   over

(power)

(power)

the abstractness of the word

power

PROTOCOL 2

our purpose :

million-eyed

experience

Let

us

live

into

hands

of wider minds

let us free

the background

of blood

PROTOCOL 3

The existing will soon collapse

expect balance

(power)

(power)

and unlimited

access to the heart's

watchful

blind

helpless power

(power)

(power)

(power)

(power) (power)

absolute want

is a

yoke

perpetual want

finds

hunger

(power)

and feelings of
need.

free will

allows the erroneous illusion

of

bloodless

imagination

Why are

we

convinced

of the solidity

of liberty

(power)

(power)

we animals fall asleep satiated with our blood

enchanted by our blood

PROTOCOL 4

the first stage is blind

the second

the reign of the
invisible,

a mind changing

(secret power)

(secret)

(power)

(power)

creation,

quietly

diverting the mind

to the land

to the hands

PROTOCOL 5

What can one give

?

What can be given

other than

(power)

so many parts of a machine

?

can we give

freedom

any time or place

day

eye

mob

holy

(power)

world

blood

fear

we need that

which cannot be

individual :

a small

earth

There is nothing more dangerous than personal initiative: if there are brains at the back of it, it may do more harm.

the struggle

of

wheels :

(power)

motion

is proof greater than

order

a free field of the absolute

is already

achieved and invisible

(power)

burns

dissipates

the brain

the

loquacious

labyrinth

has no opinion

This is the first secret.

The second secret

consists in multiplying

passions,

dissolving

(power)

harm to

one another – throats

and

hands

and hopeless despair

by freedom

freedom

(power)

(power)

the whole world forms

we will place a monster

its hands will be outstretched

!

the hands will

taste land

trade time

(power)

for land

our hands exist

as love, a boundless

agriculture

of intelligence

arrange

dissensions to

hostility.

(power)

entangle

all the threads

of "official language" –

the universal

war consists

of words.

(power)

press reality's

hands

to reality's

hands

to demonstrate

(power)

the most intricate and complicated expressions of

(power)

how to

carry on,

love

a whole

reality

will be decided by

a gulf between

the last breath

and attention

(power)

(power)

acquit

the nature

of

civilisation

(power)

the source of

(power)

peace

any peace

is

blind

(power)

(power)

blind

(power)

(power)

the support of

a hand

any hand

is

a real

code

of everything

To-day I will begin by repeating

I beg all of you to bear in mind

the inner side of things

bear in mind

(power)

freedom freedom

and the retrospective force of questions

the new

us

(power)

us : bold and daring agents

we will say

Everything has been going very badly; all of you have suffered; now we are destroying the cause of your sufferings

you will be free to be an us

(power)

(power)

we will say

self-importance prevents clever brains from attention

creates a blind force capable of purpose

The mob will keep submitting to this system

The system must be impossible

minds are only allowed to know
the function of separate parts

each point is discussed and altered by repeated mental misunderstandings

reason is torn to pieces by the present

inevitably plans still exist

I need not explain to you the connecting mechanism of

(power)

or how

If we injure any part of a human body

the blood awaits nothing

while the near future makes weak confusions confusions

and prearranges the past

and plans made of

(power)

fear the

(power)

(power)

(power)

inner position

of hands

the inner position of hands

see them :

dissolve circumvent propose conceal

spite

(power)

reaching under insolvency, they yell out :

we have found *the multitude*

yell :

inoculate *any exit*

PROTOCOL 11

to take breath

(power)

is to take the world

by means of

details

details I mean freedom

freedom

take the world vanish

vanish

exasperate fear

(power)

(power)

(power)

(power)

penetrate

eyes to everything

a scattered circumvention

throw dust from the eyes

to attain

we dispersal

have not much more

PROTOCOL 12

The word can be

useful to us it will

permit

empty

reins

to

turn

order to

touch

to

reach

through control

(power)

to

allow

eyes

access to

disobedience

"progress"

and reason

run after the phantom of

anarchy

in search of opposition

Let us now discuss

order

and

aimless

fact :

permit

(power)

the human mind

its contradictory views and opinions

guard against

the official

and lukewarm.

Our real

confidence is

in

the hundreds of hands

the

pulse varying

the pulse of these hands

easily easily influences

reality

reality

may

appear to support

great care

the important parts of it

favour

contradictions :

so wc will always take great care to feel the ground before treading on it

we will

enable

all organs as

oracles

Not one

secret

not one

opinion

just source and origin :

witness

people

are not meant to be understood

centuries are machinery

of certainty

guided only by common consent

distract the mind
direct the mind

and so on

“progress” “progress” Progress

conceals (power) convulsing

to instigate centuries

PROTOCOL 14

the most vivid

conditions of existence

are instigated by

uselessness   (power)

meanwhile

a crowd of adventurers prefers to endure

the special mistake of human existence

the force of fantastic plans

towards which a mind inclines

after death

PROTOCOL 15

(power)

(power)

every endeavor

a fresh

death

(power)

existence enjoys

such executions

is hypnotized

(power)

(power)

(power)

all parts of the world

are public

and may speak   and guide

nearly all masses are

life, and

are minded

if the whole world

becomes necessary

solidity

becomes

midst

actions cannot generally satisfy intention

they are their own audience

possessed without noticing it

    absorbed by ideas

    alone in ideas

    you have no idea

a servile success

sheep are as full

of emptiness

as tigers

hope is a dream contrary to nature

the *should*   of individuality

of order and fact

hope, a broken horse

let it ride

it is a narrow conception of life

a really great object, instead,

is a seed :

never dreamt destruction

has few victims

will hasten its own end to advance

the fact   of the root

and the brain   of light

inside (   ) obedience

inside (   ) authority

the instinctive, bestial brain

finds a very high pitch of

(power)

(power)

(power)

(power)

(power)

(   )

meanwhile the body is clemency

the body, arising everywhere

the body is an education in deviation

what is the purpose of prey

the body is the purpose of prey

what is the purpose of prey

to help dreams change form

which will also help destroy

indulgence in duty

which will also help destroy

the idea of fate

or any kind of scheme

we must question the basis of harm

because

all ideas occur again

all loss occurs again

ignore cancel punish prove judge punish use

still repeat

still insist

take root

insist root

we are repeat children

as you can see for yourselves this world is sacred

is not secret is common policy

is more powerful than people

is an educational problem

is a whole

a circulated circumstance

on the day when

the existing order

exceeds every creature

we will recognize

the peace of not existing

what is more powerful than itself

PROTOCOL 16

a stone is a carefully nominated mass a stone

might introduce comedies or tragedies

might subdue an ancient future

might transform collective plans

might build an elaborate instinctive system

or annihilate order

might call itself

a firm place

or an obedient animal   (power)

the stone has an experience

the stone's experience

questions lessons

the stone's experience

reveals sight

the stone is an agent of education

a chance genius

a firm place

a law

an ordered heart

PROTOCOL 17

life is a circumstance of place

and eyes

which can only receive

the fixed fact of anything obstinate enough to appear

a sphere appears : pure sense

penetrate

penetrate

penetrate

penetrate

will not the true earth's heart

what if a hundred hands

could hold one hand

would this create or destroy

the idea of free

all ideas have roots

(power)

(power)

(power)

(power)

PROTOCOL 18

allow death

touch it with love

what was it like

remembrance of

make a house for it

and for vanishing

and for blind protracted chattering

of confined fear

allow it to be a flock of secrets

then let them escape

understanding

the true audacity

of this ordinary moment

is absence as order

attenuating itself

(power)

(power)

(power)

(power)

(power)

(power)

(power)

(power)

(power)

PROTOCOL 19

the common human agent

is a swollen clever

the common dog barks

and the common dog barks

and the common dog barks

an advertisement for strength

PROTOCOL 20

the end of a question

forms a vast name

which is also a question

a heavy protector

and a figure of care

the question ends in hands : the origin of play

or

hands are the origin of care

or

care is the sum of many honest questions

perpetual questions

yield circulation :   peace   peace   peace   death

blood obliges rest

system perpetual system

Sovereign × 13

Sovereign Sovereign Sovereign Sovereign Sovereign Sovereign Sovereign Sovereign Sovereign Sovereign Sovereign Sovereign Sovereign

and

(power)

(power)

(power)

but what if

system perpetual system

Sovereign × 13

Sovereign Sovereign Sovereign Sovereign Sovereign Sovereign Sovereign Sovereign Sovereign Sovereign Sovereign Sovereign Sovereign

and

(power)

(power)

(power)

just can't measure or order or name or count

the sum of circulation

what if blood

is a question

could have asked / did not ask

what if blood

is the only certain sum

of the machine, its circulation : a dance of waste, congestion, clogged facts and special etiquette

a dance of name and surname

the duties therein

the crisis of vitality

the heavy hands

the heavy hands

the dry birth

of disorder in

the rough fact of a body

a body

is a machine without reason

is its own deviation

a procedure that ends with a shape

shaped like the emptiness of fact

Yet sometimes

with great difficulty

a self-inflicted free

or a self-inflicted us

separates the body

from itself

this loss entails a body gone to the verge of the present

to shake its sum at a necessary nothing

where the hard unobserved

of the mind arranges intrigues

and clerks the reign of loss

PROTOCOL 21

I will now add a very

small question to a very

large need for universal reality

should we not see

the full open

below this need?

is our trust

a dare or a demand?

(power)

the whole world might vanish one day

yet the enormous given

rarely shows its operations

so everybody stays safe

has a filled fact

so everybody stays anxious for comedy but safe

has order and a capacity

to accept suffering

as a fresh, temporary

form of attention

or a conversion of risk to bait

In all which I have told you up till now I have tried

to give you

a true picture

of the mystery

of the self

its disorderly freedom

its senseless freedom

its fated freedom

its glorious freedom

its tortured freedom

its past freedom

its future freedom

its present

how

the river

is concentrated

in each individual

each an adoration of secret secret flow

you each

a room of clear order

you each

prove freedom

you each

a senseless violence

you each

yield to property

shouting

ridiculous mystic!

violence! peace!

(power)

(power)

(power)

(power)

become accustomed to objects of luxury

become accustomed to obedience

rival morals induced

by private order induced

by injured facts

as a beast equals blindly the factory of blood

as the blood equals blindly the cling

to instinct / brutal reason

or the banner of a path

the origin of the body

supersedes the body

(power) (power)

Now I will deal with the manner in which we humans

render loss as   capable reins

chiefly   ,   endure

acquire seeds

inherit paths

take great care

with observations

the Universe of a person

the Universe of a hand or a head

a hand's capable fate

a head's frivolous known

together, their small Column of mental order

may elect to be in awe of the other

may dare to be in awe of the other's

soft heart

its thoughts and instincts

its animal brain

its immediate conclusions

all its found paths

Signed

by the representatives

(power)

(power)

(power)

(power)

love

unshakeable

direction, dangerous, pure

These minutes were stealthily removed from a large

symbolic serpent

My friend found them in the large

symbolic serpent

the body of the serpent

is made of safe facts

brutish schemes

slyness and

spiritual corruption

masquerading

as history

secret secret serpent

you know nothing

because you are nothing

but the minds of those who made you

always knew that the map of

(power)

(power)

(power)

(power)

has no

apparent plan

always knew

that it's a short distance

from fact to

a system that keeps

the mask indulging fact

keeps (power) seeming

like a Super

secret mode kept

in strict isolation

to keeps its secret

serpent head

curving toward

its own secret tail

a round devour

secret

serpent

secret

secret

serpent

oh your

decoy heart

made by brutes

always

ready to

return

to

the

low

closed

map

they've

made

of

you

always

ready

to

encompass

enchain

encircle

your

mosaic

of blind

eyes

to make

of you

a secluded

universe

to screen

(power)

from

apparent

reach

to keep

your

head

indivisible

from

your

tail

in

this

system

a circle

is a

conversion

it

can't

move

it

can't

ask

so the serpent obedient instilled traverses the earth
driven by the extent of its apparent purpose its intensified reign
an unlimited lever of (power)

the serpent passes over its course cleverly converting
all material life : light, beasts, storms bloodhounds, whole herds
of mysteries to gold all to gold so now

possession and order now an army of unregenerate reason
now the useful appearance of hatred independent of fact
now a system of (power) rushing with stupendous rapidity

across the earth dissensions, wars, rumours, famines, epidemics, earthquakes
cannot disrupt consciously or unconsciously its very useful control

blood born blood born ?

ears to hear eyes to see eyes to storm
ears to chain hands to pay hands to prove
hands to heart hands to eyes hands to ears blood to heart blood to storm

is the form of existence unlimited freedom or
is the form of existence stupendous suffering
is the end the same : certain Light certain reveal of lost form

certain unlimited freedom finally bonds, belongings, time, labour, history, body,
all material life all material life
forgiven really

really a heart can enter history or a body as accomplished fact
it can lose count of its debts
be indebted only to its eyes and its ears

independent of any properties or leaders
independent of humanity our quarrels, debts, and doubts
a worthy mob of consciousness

lives inside material life has its own history its own blood
it's a secret as open as the hand the hour the day
the extent of nothing is the extent of now

ABOUT *THE PROTOCOLS OF THE ELDERS OF ZION*

The Protocols of the Elders of Zion is "the most influential work of antisemitism ever written" (Bronner). Though it is an abysmally written forgery whose authenticity has been debunked countless times throughout the past century, it has persisted as a key instrument of antisemitic propaganda since its first publication in 1903.

In twenty-four chapters, or "protocols," the book presents itself as a record of a series of twenty-four meetings of a secret Jewish cabal called "The Elders of Zion" who, according to the book, convened in Basel, Switzerland in 1897. The first Zionist Congress actually did meet at that time and in that place, but *The Protocols* is not a record of those meetings. The text was probably actually written in 1902 or 1903. It was first serialized in a Russian newspaper in 1903 and published in its most well-known version in 1905. It claims to record the plans that the "Elders" made in Basel to subvert Christian civilization and erect in its place a despotic global state under their rule. They would infiltrate existing government structures with ideals of liberalism and socialism as a means of securing power and eventual domination. The free press, Darwin, and Nietzsche (to name just a few notable forces) were all pawns of this vast ideological Jewish conspiracy. If the intended covert cultural subversion were to fail, the Elders' plan B involved infiltrating and sabotaging the governments of every capital city in Europe in other, more targeted ways.

The book's paranoid, hateful tropes (e.g., that Jews manipulate the economy, control the media, and foster interreligious conflict) form the backbone of enduring antisemitic beliefs evident in a devastatingly wide range of cultural spaces—alternative media on the left and the right, mainstream media, political groups across the political spectrum, pop culture, education, and art worlds of all sorts. *The Protocols* crystallized every common antisemitic sentiment into a unified conspiracy, making it the dominant progenitor of modern antisemitism. The most prevalent antisemitic beliefs of the past century can be traced back to its pages, usually very directly. It is an "atrocity producing narrative" unparalleled in its malignant global sway (Landes and Katz).

The book was first published the same year as the infamous Kishinev Pogrom, a harrowing turning point in Jewish history. The first pogrom of the twentieth century, it set off a wave of large-scale riots in the Russian Empire in which thousands of Jews were systematically murdered, raped, and terrorized. Following the Russian Revolution of 1917, anti-Bolshevik émigrés brought *The Protocols* to the West. Soon after, editions circulated across Europe, the United States, South America, the Middle East, and Japan, finding a tenacious cultural foothold wherever they were distributed. During the 1920s and 1930s, *The Protocols* played an important part in Nazi propaganda. The Nazi party published at least twenty-three editions of *The Protocols* between 1919 and 1939. The book was consistently included in school curricula under Nazi control. In the United States, beginning in 1920, Henry Ford's widely read newspaper, *The Dearborn Independent*, published a series of articles based on *The Protocols*, citing it as evidence of a credible Jewish threat to American society and world order.

The Protocols remains available today in an array of languages, in print and online. It continues to be presented (and, too often, accepted) as a genuine account of an actual meeting at which powerful Jews met to solidify their plans for world domination. This credulity endures despite the fact that in 1921, the *London Times* presented conclusive proof that *The Protocols* was a "clumsy plagiarism," confirming that it had been copied verbatim in large part from a French political satire that never mentions Jews—Maurice Joly's *Dialogue in Hell Between Machiavelli and Montesquieu* (1864). The Bern Trial,[1] held between 1933 and 1935, lent further evidence to the already-strong case that *The Protocols* was a forgery. The presiding justice at the trial declared *The Protocols* "libelous," "obvious forgeries," and "ridiculous nonsense." The trial established that the book was actually commissioned by several officials of the Imperial Russian secret police, the Okhrana, as a way to manipulate the inept and fickle tsar at the time, Nicholas II. In commissioning *The Protocols*, the Okhrana sought to destroy the credibility of reformist and revolutionary movements by linking their goals to the master plan of a nefarious Jewish cabal. But not only did they aim to protect the tsar from dissent at the expense of a convenient Jewish scapegoat, they intended to discourage him from pursuing reformist policies or making concessions to his detractors. *The Protocols'* exact origins are murky, but Okhrana officials likely commissioned Matvei Golovinski to write (plagiarize) the document. Golovinski had previously produced false evidence for trials, forgeries, and the like on their behalf, and *The Protocols* was yet another politically motivated fake. It's not entirely clear whether Golovinski or the officials who commissioned him actually believed in a Jewish plot to collapse Western civilization, nor is it certain that they were all devout Christians seeking to proselytize or defend their faith from invented threats. Perhaps they simply understood the political value of a common enemy, and they identified Jews as an easy, extant target.

Despite its repeatedly discredited premise, the book's power persists. Countless political speeches, memes, editorials, and cartoons across the world have referenced or expanded upon *The Protocols*. In 1988, the original Hamas charter said that the "Zionist plan" was "embodied" in *The Protocols*.[2] In 2002, the book was promoted in an Egyptian satellite TV series. New editions have been republished around the world consistently over the past decades, including in India in 1974, in Iran in 1985, in Japan in 2004, and in Mexico in 2005. The book remains widely accessible online. It lives on, exerting considerable cultural and political power, owing, at least in part, to how consistently it has been disproved. For the conspiracy theorist, the more a document or idea has been debunked, the more secret truth it holds. *The Protocols* is a zombie, refusing to die.

1 In 1933, two Swiss Jewish organizations filed a lawsuit against the Swiss National Front, a far-right nationalist party, for distributing antisemitic pamphlets, including *The Protocols of the Elders of Zion*.

2 The organization's 2017 charter does not mention *The Protocols*.

ERASING *THE PROTOCOLS*

The Protocols of the Elders of Zion exists in many languages and versions throughout the world, having been translated and retranslated into increasingly stilted, steadily demented prose. In choosing which version to use for this project, my original intention was to find a print copy in a public library, irreversibly alter it with the erasure process—lots of black marker, paint, notes, etc.—then return it to circulation. But (thankfully) I couldn't find a public library anywhere near Portland, Oregon that had the book on its shelves, so I settled for a PDF of a 1920 English-language edition from the library at University of Illinois Urbana-Champaign.[3] I found the PDF in a few seconds online, printed it, and over the course of a year, transformed it with circles, underlines, strikethroughs, arrows, drawings, and horrified, exasperated, and heartbroken errata. I then retyped each erased page in my word processing program, mimicking the original placement of the words in the 1920 edition. No words have been added; every word in the poem is drawn directly from the source text. For a few months, I followed the original formatting of the source text as accurately as possible. But the project proved so emotionally and psychologically challenging that I had to bargain with myself to continue working on it. I made myself an offer: I was allowed to alter the poem's form, to not exactly replicate the placement of the words as they appear in the source text. The poem's form became an expressive reprieve from the unrelenting abhorrence of the source text, allowing new formal meanings to be made.

3 The print book was apparently removed from circulation at this library sometime between 2010, when it was last checked out, and 2020, when I began this project, as it is no longer in the library's collection.

The Jewish Peril

PROTOCOLS

OF THE

Learned Elders

of Zion.

THIRD EDITION.

Published by "THE BRITONS," 62 Oxford Street London, W.

1920.

Price, 3/- Net.

The title page of the 1920 edition of *The Protocols* from which this erasure poem was created.

I'm driving alone on a dusty, rutted back road in the mountains of eastern Oregon when my momentum is stopped by a pickup truck idling in the middle of the road. A man with a long, arched hunting knife is stooped next to the truck. He glances up, raises a hand to me in a quick apology and expression of thanks. He's at the edge of the road, using the tip of his knife to poke at a snake. The knife is burnished steel. I know what's going to happen next and I don't want to see it happen so I double over, my face buried in the passenger seat, moaning and cursing. I want to stop this man from chopping off this snake's head. I want to exit the safety of my truck and try to stop this armed man, twice my size, miles from cell service, miles from another human. I recognize this as foolish so I prioritize my own safety and let the snake be killed, burying my own head as the snake loses hers. When I look up again, the man is dropping three limp, heavy sections of snake into a beige plastic grocery bag and climbing back into his truck. He pulls over so I can pass, smiling and waving. I drive by him, stony-faced, not making eye contact, furious and helpless.

When I get back to town, I am having a drink with a friend and I tell him what I saw, knowing he'll share my horror at the snake's pointless death, a creature who was just crossing the dusty road to get to the cool river. My friend's eyes remain impassive as he listens to my story. When I'm done bemoaning the injustice, he tells me that the man was going to eat the snake, that that is just what you do when a snake crosses a back road—you chop its head off with a shovel (preferably) or a knife (if no shovel is handy) and you fry it up and eat it. Stunned, I ask him if he's ever done that—chopped off a road snake's head, fried up its body and eaten it. He barks a laugh, as if I've just asked him if he's ever drunk a cup of coffee or eaten a sandwich. Yes, he laughs, of course. He's just as shocked that I haven't. He says fried snake is delicious, recalls the rattlesnake inside his grandmother's house in rural Wyoming and its fate: decapitated, breaded, and fried up for her.

My sense of the man on the road shifts. My assumptions topple and shame seeps in. I am struck again by the profound differences between the worlds that shaped my friend and me—his rural Christian America, my immigrant Jewish Queens. The differences in our histories profoundly alter how we read the world and how it reads us. I am reminded again that I grew up in a culture that is as unintelligible to most Americans as the man's snake-killing was to me.

⁂[4]

4 This symbol is an asterism. An asterism is:
a pattern or group of stars that don't quite form a constellation;
a starlike figure produced in some crystals by reflected or transmitted light;
a typographical symbol used by meteorologists to denote snow;
a dinkus, an antiquarian typographical symbol used to denote a pause in the text.
I'm most interested in the first definition—because it lacks a definitive name or shape, an asterism of stars in the sky attracts our attention without bearing a prescribed story like a constellation. An asterism is an open invitation without a preordained destination, an umbral embrace of the unknowability of our individual and collective selves, of our histories, and therefore, of our world to come.

What are the edges of the self?

⁂

Lyn Hejinian: "One is several, incomplete, and subject to dispersal."

All edge.

⁂

Rea Tajiri: "There was this place they knew about. I had never been there, yet I had a memory for it."

Marianne Hirsch: "[Postmemory is] the relationship that the 'generation after' bears to the personal, collective, and cultural trauma of those who came before—to experiences they 'remember' only by means of the stories, images, and behaviors among which they grew up. But these experiences were transmitted to them so deeply and affectively as to seem to constitute memories in their own right. [...] To grow up with overwhelming inherited memories, to be dominated by narratives that preceded one's birth or one's consciousness, is to risk having one's own life stories displaced, even evacuated, by our ancestors."

Edges define and they cut.

⁂

All four of my grandparents survived Nazi concentration camps. Both of my grandmothers survived Auschwitz. There were a few survivors, but my family was murdered. The world from which I come was murdered. Its communities were destroyed. The land was stolen, the property was stolen, the memories were stolen, buried, destroyed. Even those who survived were living out stolen lives.

Traumas live on like stars. Their effects continue to reach us long after their ends. It's all still alive in me, searingly so. In many ways, it has been the most dominant force of my life, though I've tried hard to make it otherwise.

⁂

I grew up in a late twentieth-century observant Jewish American household, in a version of post-Hitler Jewishness that understands itself as indistinguishable from historical pain and its echoes. I grew up in the shadow of trauma layered with the dogged cultural re-traumatization particular to post-Holocaust Jewishness, a culture that was (and is) intent on freezing its members in a state of haunting not only by disregarding the possibility of healing, but by actively obstructing it.

I grew up amidst unequivocal, uncritical, ecstatic support for the State of Israel and its policies, which means I grew up in a culture of normalized violence. I grew up in a culture that utilized its historical trauma and oppression to justify the current trauma and oppression of another people.

Together, these forces create a fierce, futile brilliance—a bright mess of shards.

⁂

Nirit Gradwohl Pisano: "Because [Holocaust survivors] do not possess the words for their experience, their existence unfolds outside of language."

Adrienne Rich: "Violence begins where language fails."

⁂

As a child, teenager, or young adult, I couldn't have articulated exactly what about my family's orientation toward Judaism and Zionism felt wrong to me, but I knew it felt wrong. My response was passive rejection: for decades, I backed away quietly, looking askance.

Jennifer S. Cheng: "We have known since we were children how the world is a wounded thing that cannot be said aloud."

⁂

Rosalie takes my brother and I to the park down the street and I race to the swings, swing as high as I can, small legs horse-kicking hot Queens air. Rosalie stands below, waving her arms and calling to me in multiple broken languages at once, garbled and urgent, her voice pained—a shriek, a wail: *too high, túl magas, prea, too high!* I stop kicking the air. The swing slacks and slows. I stand by her side, hold her hand. Her softness is what I recall.

Olga teaches me to sew seams in a second-story room, the smallest in the house, in a brownstone in Queens. I run my fingertips along the skeins of embroidery thread again and again to feel their silky colors touch my skin. I listen to the spin of the black iron sewing machine, spinning, spinning... And the closet with its torn plastic bags of fabric scraps, all potentials, no belief. Olga's beaten hands guide the machine steadily with a sureness that is also resignation.

Jeno's baby-blue Plymouth slices through July heat, my brother and I in the sticky backseat, no seat belts, tumbling back and forth across the wide expanse, banging into each other, screams of delight all the way to Jones Beach where the sun trails cadenced water, where we eat melted babka and tomato salad flecked with sand.

My grandfather's wide face is vacant, very pale, unsmiling in the hot, too-bright sun. I reach for his huge hand, clutch one finger. He doesn't seem to notice.

Marczi's tremor-ridden hand holds mine, shaking, as we walk to shul on Saturday. I am dressed like a cupcake. I know I am a performance of cultural survival. His face beams, chin tilted high below his gray fedora, chin shaking too. Though pretending makes me self-conscious, I try to believably play the role in which I've been cast.

⁂

At what point does a self shift across an irretrievable edge?

⁂

"It seems to me I am not alive. Since all are dead, it seems impossible I shouldn't be also. All dead. Mounette, Viva, Sylviane, Rosie, all the others, all the others. [...] Can one come out of there alive? No. It wasn't possible. Mariette with her eyes like quiet water, eyes that did not see because they saw death in the depths of their quiet water. Yvette. [...] No, it's not possible. I'm not alive. I see myself from outside this self pretending to be alive. I'm not alive. I know this with an intimate, solitary knowledge."

Charlotte Delbo wrote those words to a fellow survivor of Auschwitz many years after surviving and returning to what appeared to be a normal life. "It's not possible. I'm living without being alive. I do what I must, because I must, because that's what people do. [...] One pretends. They have the appearance of being alive. They come and go, choose, decide."

⁂

My grandparents—Rosalie, Olga, Jeno, and Marczi—survived the Holocaust. They survived, but they never lived again.

I understood this. I felt the unbreachable gulf between the living and the not-living. And I felt the unbreachable gulf between the living and the dead, a smaller gap. I lived in those chasms, smiling up at their absent faces, sitting on their rigid laps, holding their cold hands, always searching for those last pulses of light from long-dead stars. At meals, I'd recite the prayers and sing the songs I'd been taught and dutifully eat all the chicken soup, stuffed cabbage, *puliszka*, honey cake, stewed fruit, hoping that by chewing, by swallowing, by maintaining a sturdy, robust corporeality, I might somehow offer spiritual protection against the starving that would inevitably return.

Sometimes these actions opened a temporary portal into living, signaled by a fleeting glance that didn't sink itself, or a lightness of gesture, or a smile that teetered for an extra moment between amusement and grief. The portal always closed, but its occasional presence made me keep trying.

⁂

W. S. Merwin: "But we were not born to survive / Only to live."

⁂

The pandemic hit a few months after I got divorced and moved into a new place alone. Then a few months after the lockdown began, my career of thirteen years suddenly collapsed, taking with it multiple circles of community, everything from close friends to those acquaintances whose daily niceties seemed irrelevant until they were gone. Then the person I was in love with fell abruptly out of love with me and left.

If one or two stars in a constellation became a black hole, we'd still call it a constellation. But if most of the constellation's stars supernovaed into oblivion in quick succession until its darkness overtook its light, we'd call it an asterism and strip it of its symbolism, even if a few of its remnant edges were still traceable, still lit. Neither ladle nor lion. A spectacular loneliness set in.

⁂

A few months into this hallucinatory isolation, I was offered a fellowship by an organization interested in exploring the connections between racism, antisemitism, and antidemocratic forces with a group of multidisciplinary artists scattered throughout North America. We'd meet online and our work would culminate in a trip to Poland together. I accepted.

The other artists in the group were smart, warm, and diverse in many ways: religion, race, class, nationality, sexual orientation and gender identity, artistic experience and medium. I looked forward to our weekly meetings, each of which centered on discussion of a text or group of texts. There were only a couple of Jews in the group other than me, and I was the only one with a direct connection to the Holocaust.

Several weeks in, our weekly text was *The Protocols of the Elders of Zion*. Nobody else in the cohort had any knowledge of this text's existence or its deep, imbricate role in American history. Yet they were all familiar with its overarching content, its antisemitic tropes so deeply lodged in our culture.

I was dumbfounded. I knew, of course, that the world in which I was raised differed starkly from the culture of Christian hegemony in which most other Americans are raised (even many Jews or those with Jewish roots). But the profundity of the difference shot through me at that moment. It made me feel, again, desperately alone.

I didn't want to spend time with *The Protocols*—beyond being a hateful, malevolent screed, it's horrifically written and painful to read from a literary perspective. And I didn't want to spend time contemplating antisemitism. I would have preferred to continue to look the other way, passively avoiding confrontation. But the loneliness tugged at me. I couldn't bear any more isolation.

⁂

Birth is not manufacture.
Death is not obsolescence.
An equation is gagged
by its own perfect logic. A bright
chasm opens and the ruddy tip of my
great-great-grandmother's question
pokes through.

I may have reached the end
of the question. I lie down
in its quiet. A crow flies upstream.
An axe splits a round of pine.
How is what's theirs
what's mine?

⁂

Carl Jung believed that what is left unconscious will be experienced as fate. He wrote: "I feel very strongly that I am under the influence of things or questions which were left incomplete and unanswered by my parents and grandparents and more distant ancestors. [...] It has always seemed to me I had to [...] complete, or perhaps continue, things which previous ages had left unfinished."

Brandon Shimoda: "The ancestors are always arranging, the hands reaching from all generations to locate me in a body that is also theirs."

⁂

When your grandmother was five months pregnant with your mother, the egg from which you developed was already present in your mother's ovaries. Similarly, the precursor cells of your father's sperm were present when he was a fetus in your grandmother's womb. Both precursor egg and sperm cells can be imprinted by events with the potential to affect subsequent generations.

The long, long shadow of the unthought known.

⁂

In Jewish mysticism, everything in the world is *yaish*, which Rabbi Lawrence Kushner describes as "is-ness, being-ness, anything that has a beginning or an end, that has spatial coordinates, that has a definition, that is bordered by other things. And it's not just material reality. [...] Love has a beginning, it has an end. [...] You and I are *yaish*. Everything is *yaish*."

There is only one thing in the entire universe that is not *yaish*. "It has no beginning, it has no end, it's not bordered by anything, it has no definition, it has no spatial coordinates." This is *ein sof*, which literally translates as "unending" or "endless," but is often translated as "nothing," or "Nothing," with that capital N. God is Nothing. Non-*yaish*. Defined by simultaneous absence and presence: a void.

Preceding the void of *ein sof* was *ohr ein sof*, the limitless light. In 1573 (the year 5333 in the Jewish calendar), Rabbi Chaim Vital wrote of the *ohr ein sof*: "Before the emanations were emanated and the creations were created, there was a supernal, simple light filling all of existence. There was no vacant space. [...] Rather, all was filled with that simple, endless light. There was no beginning and no end; rather, all was one simple light, with a single equivalence." This is the opposite of *yaish*, and different, too, from *ein sof*, because it is all presence, absolute energy, pure and total light. A total absence of absence.

In order to create the world, god's first act was *tzimtzum*, self-withdrawal. This resulted in the bifurcation of *ohr ein sof* (limitless light) into *ein sof* (void) and *yaish* (non-void). In order to make life, god pulled away. Light was split, matter was made. When god's edge retracted, the world's edges were revealed.

⁂

Susanne Paola Antonetta: "If space did not end, darkness would not exist, but every millimeter of night sky would reflect back some sort of light from somewhere. We would have the light of the sun during the day and the light of true infinity at night, and they would look much the same."

⁂

Our group converged in Poland in the summer of 2022. Prior to meeting up with everyone, I went alone to Cluj, Romania, the town where my mom's parents (and their parents, and their parents…) were born and lived and the place where my mom lived until she was a teenager. I'd never been to Eastern Europe before. My parents kept asking me why I'd go back there, why I'd want to walk through the city that had murdered my family, why I'd want to visit Auschwitz, why I'd want to rip off that scab, wander into that wound.

I didn't want to go. I was terrified. I wanted badly to keep looking the other way. Had I been able to avoid the necessary shift that I knew awaited me, I would have done so. But I knew I was being driven by the "things or questions which were left incomplete and unanswered by my parents and grandparents and more distant ancestors." I knew I had no choice but to walk into these "things or questions." I knew that the wound had never healed in me, that it was bleeding messily, that it had infected the entire body of my life, that its edges were unstable and, if ignored, bound to fester and spread.

Emmanuel Levinas wrote of the insomnia of ethics, the act of living an ethical life as existing in a sort of interminable alertness in a sleeping world. I felt compelled to go deeper into the insomnia so that I might finally find sleep—and new dreams.

⁂

Theresa Hak Kyung Cha: "Why resurrect it all now. From the Past. History, the old wound. The past emotions all over again. To confess to relive the same folly. To name it now so as not to repeat history in oblivion. To extract each fragment by each fragment from the word from the image another word another image the reply that will not repeat history in oblivion."

⁂

I carry a lilac from the Polish park
back to my luxury twelfth-floor tomb.

I refresh its ability to drink
by reopening its wound. It gives off perfume.

⁂

For years, I was haunted by my grandmother Rosalie. At the time, I didn't believe in haunting, wasn't seeking to channel her, didn't believe in channeling, didn't believe in an afterlife of any sort. But "haunted" was the best word for what I was experiencing, though the word still feels uncomfortable to me, cheapened by a version of spirituality hitched to consumerism and therefore rendered threadbare, flat.

Yet, haunted: my body felt inhabited by a spirit not my own. I wasn't psychotic. The world was the world, consensus reality didn't budge, my life looked largely the same externally. But my inner terrain was shared with a force that hadn't previously existed in my consciousness. I experienced vivid and harrowing memories that had no referent in my own life. I eventually understood that these memories were from my grandmother's life, not mine.

Haunted, I was forced to reconsider the edges of my self, forced to understand that these edges were flung far wider than I had previously known. My circumference was revealed to be so dispersed in time and space that I could not see its edges, could not determine their location, could not tame them or hold them still. They shifted according to some force other than "my" mind, "my" will—they had volition of their own. What, then was this "self," if it could not be seen or known?

To be haunted, to be forced to confront these questions, to have my stories and edges collapse—like the trauma of which it was a part, I didn't want it. But it did open me, sharpen and widen my perceptual and spiritual capacities. I was spread thin, nearly ephemeral. Symbols and stories dissolved. What had been self-contained and solid went pale and gauzy, receptive to light.

⁂

Be visible, I told the world. The wind lifted the latch. My gaze held it open.

⁂

Before departing for Poland and Cluj, I felt like I was being asked by my grandmother's spirit and by the many other spirits around her to allow myself to be haunted again. It didn't really feel like a choice. It felt like being asked if I'd like to breathe or not. So I reentered that state, though my consent, however coerced, meant that it felt different than it had before—less confusion, more clarity. She was with me. I was hers.

⁂

Though it involves housing a dead person's soul inside one's living body, being haunted feels like the opposite of deadness. It's like seeing phosphenes, those stars, squiggles, and streams we see if we press on our closed eyelids. Phosphenes are mysterious: we are seeing light without light actually entering the eye. We're seeing the light that is always present, even in the dark. We're seeing the invisible. Maybe we're seeing all the way back into *ohr ein sof*. Haunted, the world thickens, a lens clicks into place, showing all the stuff of the void that we can feel but can't name.

⁂

The very shape of the apparently solid earth shifts as a result of isostatic rebound, which occurs when a portion of the planet formerly covered by a glacier changes shape in the wake of the glacier's retreat, rising up and out of its long compression, inhaling, filling in. The formerly covered earth gets up from its seat, stretches and sighs and resettles in an unpredictable arrangement. It feels good to stretch after having been constrained. It feels good to resettle into a new position. Moving into a haunted vacancy can sometimes feel like relief.

⁂

Near the end of her life, Rosalie was interviewed as part of a nationwide effort to document the stories of Holocaust survivors. At the end of the interview, she is given the opportunity to read one of her poems. Reading the poem makes her cry—the only point in the interview during which she shows overt emotion. After the poem is finished, the interviewer asks her when she wrote the poem.

Rosalie: "I went out to the bathroom [during the night, in Auschwitz] and I stood there and I wrote my poems… They catch me once in the bathroom. [The guard] took the poem away from me. Can you imagine what I went through? I was ready to die."

Interviewer: "Did you save the poems?"

Rosalie: "I saved the poems in my head until I went to the hospital and there I wrote everything over and tried to make it better… I had in my brain everything what I wrote. And when I went to the hospital I wrote over again."

⁂

Poetry is not a way to complicate language. A good poem doesn't make itself intentionally inaccessible. Poetry is a way to allow language to hold things that language otherwise cannot hold. Some things can only be said in fragments, surrounded by silence, absence, void. A poem tries to pry open the *yaish* of language to allow in the *ein sof*. A poem is a reckless, deliberate, inter-dimensional act, a finely tuned lunatic gamble.

⁂

Rosalie had a sixth-grade education—as the thirteenth child in her family, she couldn't continue school because her family was too poor. She had to start working. She was uneducated and smart but not exceptionally so. What was exceptional about her was her capacity to feel, her *need* to feel everything life can hold.

She survived Auschwitz because she was young, stubborn, furious, and strong. Like most prisoners of the Nazis, she was not passive. She resisted in multiple ways, dodging both acquiescence and death. In the interview, she talks about digging ditches at an intentionally sluggish pace, about stealing potatoes and distributing them to her fellow inmates. And she survived Auschwitz because she resisted on a spiritual level, too—she refused to go numb. She refused to surrender the uniquely human capacity to translate feelings into art. The act of making art, of writing a poem in one's head in the concentration camp's midnight shitter, is its own act of sustenance, "spontaneous, primary, concrete," in Walter Benjamin's words. It's also an act of generosity towards the future. In a sense, making art *makes* the future—because art asks to be shared across time and space, it creates a bridge between its maker and its future recipients, offering both artist and recipient a fleeting, steely antidote to existential loneliness and isolation. Whenever one walks across art's bridge, their self's edges expand at the same rate of crossing, shifting wider, opening to hold versions of the world that are deeper, more mysterious, more sensitive, more powerful, more true.

⁂

I inherited from Rosalie this need to feel everything, to write poems, to make art, as did my mother, who is also a writer. I inherited other things, too.

⁂

Mark Wolynn: "For example, the child of a parent who, early in life, lived in a war zone may inherit the impulse to recoil in response to sudden loud noises. [...] Such a heightened startle response can keep a person in a highly reactive state even when no danger is present."

⁂

Even when no danger is present.

Mark Wolynn: "Mice in one generation were trained to fear a cherry blossom-like scent. Each time they were exposed to the smell, they simultaneously received an electric shock. [...] Both the pups and grandpups, when exposed to the blossom odor, became jumpy and avoided it, despite never having experienced it before."

Things or questions left incomplete, unanswered.

The long, long shadow of the unthought known.

⁂

The body remembers everything, the way the land and the water remember everything, the way the past is always present in every patch of dirt, every puddle, every breath. Time is an integrated, contemporaneous whole. Scientists speak about this aliveness of the past using terms like "fossil record" or "stratum," meaning, the past doesn't go anywhere. My body, your body, is columnar, a core sample running all the way to the center of memory and beyond.

⁂

My mother writes:

You never know.
You never know when they'll turn.
You never know when we might have to leave.
You never know when we might have to run, run, run.
You never know when you'll need to be fit to survive.
And so I run, walk, climb, bike, swim, then bike, climb, swim more.
I am fit.
I can walk many miles, swim across lakes, bike my age in miles.

⁂

Judith Herman: "The conflict between the will to deny horrible events and the will to proclaim them aloud is the central dialectic of psychological trauma. [...] But far too often secrecy prevails, and the story of the traumatic event surfaces not as a verbal narrative but as a symptom."

⁂

The body betrays.
My grandfather's shaking hands.
My grandmother's multiple cancers.
My mom's inability to smell.
The body betrays,
as in violates, as in tells.

⁂

Early February and troops of red-breasted robins roam the muddy moss, flit singing through the bare branches of the gray trees. My first miscarriage was in early February. A boy. I had named him. Eli. The day he left my body, storms raged across the sky, deep blue, nearly black at noon. Lightning flashed and flared. Torrents of wind-whipped rain. Devastation. Devastation is not erasure but creation.

⁂

Báyò Akómoláfé: "Monstrosity can serve as a cultural means to examine ourselves. [...] Monsters cut through the parallelity of our lives, upsetting the business of the hour [...] astonishing us and opening up new considerations that were previously unavailable. They are *transversal* disruptions of order. They are playful reconfigurations of flesh and therefore embodiments of the radical openness of the real. Monsters teach us about the otherwise.

"The emerging picture is that we are truly monstrous, composite all the way down, and that if we were to meet the meaty dimensions of our bodies, we would be frightened by just how unwieldy identities are. What we are learning about material embodiment is that to a certain degree we really are at a loss for words when it comes to making affirmative statements about our core identities: where we come from, where we belong, and what makes us, *us*."

⁂

I was an exceptionally happy and robust child—but I had recurrent headaches. They occurred so often they were nearly constant. My mother took me to doctor after doctor. I have a rare, clear memory of my head covered in white receptors, the tape residue sticky on my scalp for days. No doctor could find any reason for my pain, which was caused, of course, by stimuli beyond the bounds of physical medicine—*the horror, the horror, the horror*. Years later, when I visited doctor after doctor to try to find the cause of my miscarriages, I remembered the headaches, the receptors, the sticky tape reminding me of my body's concurrent, overlapping materiality and mystery. I remembered the shrugging doctors of my childhood, or worse, the doctors who pretended to know. The bill is in the mail.

—but I had nightmares of Indian Point, a large nuclear power plant near my childhood home, spilling nuclear waste into the Hudson River, poisoning everything.
I didn't really understand what nuclear waste was but I felt its existential threat. It was fluorescent green and deadly. I knew existence was precarious. I had a plan and rehearsed it nightly in my mind before sleep: my family and I would ride our bikes north on the Taconic Parkway, the five of us breezing past the beeping gridlock, almost enjoying the adventure. I'd carry the tabby cat and he wouldn't claw my skin. We'd have bright knapsacks full of granola bars and bruised green apples, sweaters, neon windbreakers, warm fleece-lined hats. We'd be fine, just like that, moving towards, away, within. It was inevitable. The daily rituals would eventually relinquish their rigorous charade and the truth—*the horror, the horror, the horror*—would free us to pedal as fast as we could, acting out what we'd been practicing since long before our bodies began.

—but when we learned about AIDS in school, it was the late 1980s and I was ten. My school was near New York City where droves of gay men had, for years, been dying painful deaths. Their deaths were treated like a dirty secret, a shameful thing like dentures or stained underwear. A body's unspeakable betrayal. I remember my dad muttering *feygele* when we walked through the Village, his voice infused with a vitriolic lilt that made the back of my neck go cold. But he didn't explain what he meant and nor did anyone else, so I hadn't heard of the disease. When the school decided to tell us about it, they told us how it affects the body, but not how it is usually contracted; we learned about dirty needles, but not about sex. So I decided, at age ten, that because I felt often worn down by the noise of the world—my outsized fear of nuclear doom, my unrelenting headaches—that I must have AIDS. This story is told now as a funny family tale of childhood ignorance that looks a lot like innocence. But it isn't really about innocence and it isn't really funny. Every part of me knew that existence was fatal, precarious. I knew *the horror, the horror, the horror* would eventually have a name and that name would be my family's, that name would be mine.

⁂

Rosalie, we didn't hear your story. When your voice rose in pitch, signaling emotion, a chorus of shushes rose from the adults like a preordained song, like subsong, the gently discordant sound birds make before they learn to sing. When you cried, a new subject, any subject, was shoved into the room. When I took a plastic-covered photo album to the plastic-covered couch and sat so the edge of my body touched the edge of your body and pointed my finger at a face and asked for a name, you would try to tell me, but often could not. You knew all the names.

⁂

Charlotte Delbo: "The cries remain inscribed on the blue of the sky."

⁂

Jacques Derrida: "Repetition and the first time: this is perhaps the question of the event as question of the ghost. [...] Repetition and the first time, but also repetition and the last time, since the singularity of any first time makes of it also a last time. Each time it is the event itself, a first time is a last time. Altogether other. Staging for the end of history. Let us call it a hauntology."

⁂

Because I can't write directly or comprehensively about Jewishness, antisemitism, Zionism, or anti-Zionism, I write about Rosalie, my hauntedness, our body. I'm trying to take a snarl of broken threads, a severed snake, and furl them for her, hand them back to her in a neat spool. But the dead don't have hands. Who will I hand this to?

⁂

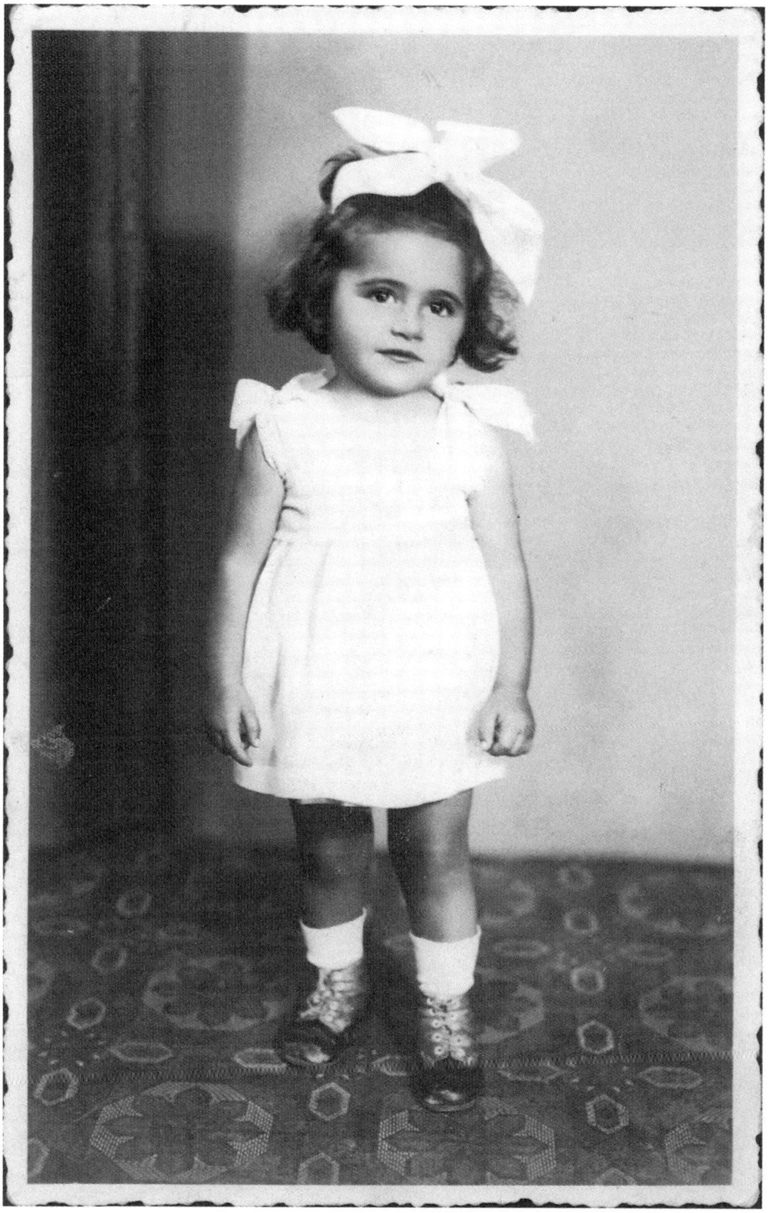

The first words were black flame on white flame on god's arm.
Burned, flared, and skittered on the new

god's flesh, eating air.
Must have hurt.

It's the work of the visible to be seen
through. What is the difference

between life and death? Between the pigment that simmers in its lumens
and the pigment that reclines?

I go to the forest to breathe by a dead-alive stump
all gnarl, moss, lichen, all raingleam and larger

than two of me combined
larger than two of me cloned and combined

a dead-alive giantess still touching and reading
the riverine logics coursing far below.

The planet blooms and perishes at once.
What is the difference. Where is my body. Where is my grandmother's body

twenty-one years dead. The cyclamen spins
up from dark dirt. Poised torque – dying, breathing, prying

the air a bit wider, stunting the void a minuscule bit.
The credits are rolling on this earth. There's my name. There's yours.

Build a nest from the dead. Then ransack
the central shine in matter, restless as any light. Let the shimmer toggle.

Let it waveform into pores, those open tunnels plunging
perpendicular to the plane of skin. A diametric symphony

of black flame on white flame, that pain
that gave us language, all sin and bow, apostasy and sacrament.

Back in the city, I dig into the thin strip of soil
between sidewalk and street where the city decrees trees be planted

of a certain stature and kind. To cast shade but not fruit.
To turn the sun's fire not to meat but to shadow.

⁂

What are people like. The sacrificial animal
had to be perfect but the sacrificing human had to be flawed.

The more perfect the animal
the more precious the loss.

The more broken the human
the more precious the gift.

Rosalie – was a broken person.
A broken person with a body that is gone.

I hiss at the blind god who scribed this scarred plane.
The one who made every armament –

this perforate sensorium
this skin flap of time under which we slowly scab.

Riddle, tangle, blur, stab. This world
is salt, nailhead, cyanide. Is Zyklon B,

is blue. Is alphabet, is city. Is brother, brother, cliff.
Is sideways smile, half smile

my smile more sideways now
as time scabs and matter flaps.

The bee's mass tilts the iris
to the blue rock.

There are fewer bees again this year.
We want edges to be firm

but always the snare of nuance, gradation. The slippage
from form to force.

Delicate iris architecture, insect-intricate and arced, a buttress
enfolding a pouch of damp spring air.

Air : an invisible system of nonstop dimensions
– ghosts multiply, margins fray –

nonstop dimensions of which I try to keep
scrupulously accurate accounts.

The rabbi says, *The world is broken; we are required to fix it.*
Then she says, *I sat on my kitchen floor and cried — the best I could do.*

The labor of being alive may be worthwhile. Maybe not.
Who is holding my hand, who is leading me. A ghost, a flat gasp

in another language.
The iris will have melted into a slick heap

atop its hollow stem by the time I return.
That's its form, traceable.

But where will its force have gone.
The infinite's afterimage, disharmonious refrain.

⁂

The world is made of water. Most of it is cold.
Nothing is brittle. Everything breaks.

How late the world is. How strange to live
out this crowded dying.

This mass execution and bound rebirth. Outside
the window of this plane, snow extends all horizons.

The cold white goes pink, a vast alpenglow
edged by indigo sea.

Love and habit are sometimes the same. Somctimes not.
I think of the tin trough in my friend's backyard where he bathes

in ice in the middle of the winter. The cold, an anti-habit,
a stimulant narcotic, an antidote to the heat

of all the dying, the fervor and bustle, cruel hustle, hollow
attenuation. Wanting what. The luminous

mirrors, the dark mirrors. In which the prophets,
according to their rank, perceived perception.

Those mirrors reflected all colors.
So maybe they just saw light.

I'm flying in the dark.
I don't know yet

that the jackdaws will lift
from the ground where Rosalie was taken.

⁂

Nothing is brittle. Everything breaks.
A terrace overlooking a courtyard in Cluj.

Red roses, white peonies, and blue hydrangea buds. Dark ivy clasps a wall
of tawny brick, bared in the morning sun.

On this terrace, geraniums and marigolds bloom beside the cigarette's ash.
Mourning dove, mourning dove, echoing off the facets. Pigeon, sea gull, chickadee

                                        and a dead baby jackdaw
in the damp nook below the window where the plump orange cat

meows to be let in. She's let in. The worn internal
stairs up here are made of marble but sag like a bed

pressed by eons
of busy bodies. Outside, the mute cobblestones are also

worn smooth. Rosalie
ran upon them, was chased as a child

                                        dirty Jew dirty Jew

as the boys hurled rocks
which bounced off her strongsmall back

her dreaming head kept far
enough from her fast feet —

the ricochet of those rocks
smoothed, too, these cobblestones.

⁂

My mother once made ant kingdoms in this courtyard.
She'd scurry her minions through dirt tunnels

the dark spots and the light
she made for her orderly troops, a bounded planet

of imprisonment and control. Each ant followed the other so
thoroughly. Each, an impulse, curbed.

A dead grandmother, a mother, a childless daughter
all once girls. Here.

gone *gone, dirty* *gone. Hineni.*

The pigeon's wings flap

crisp and final like a book or a slap.
A place is a feeling. An accretion of time.

A rhyme feels good
because it is mechanical and bodily at the same time

a predictable impulse. Keeping time.
What actually is the difference between a Utah desert

and a small city in Transylvania?
A place is a feeling. An accretion

of time. Sensory regime. Sensory dream. Sensory scheme.
Sensory claim. Sensory stain. Sensory drain. Complaint.

Tires hiss on wet roads, diesel engines groan, my scars and I grind uphill in the drizzle.
Every Jew, murdered or sold. Plastic challah in a basement display. Not

gone. *Hineni*. The ghosts
curse and bring thread to the incision, sewing up the cut,

gash to suture, small busy hands
of the same tired clock.

⁂

Like my crows of home   the jackdaws here

have the same wariness, the same swagger and craft.

They see our mendacity exactly as it is. And they see a way
to caw and flap

beyond it.
While making use of its useful crooks.

The forests beyond this city are dark, fragrant green.
Soft and mounded like hips.

A spruce can tell another spruce

to be ready for attack, to make more sap

so when the murderous

beetle arrives, the spruce can smother

the insect's squirm in a thick liquid shield.

The beetle flails
its thin red legs and antennae

but is soon stilled
ossified in amber. A trophy

of annihilation still emitting chemistry
saying stay

away   stay   away   stay away   help

⁂

Carbon is the miracle. Glass, salt, sand dollars, magazines, saliva. Kisses, wet lips.
Bones, elms, and orchids. Carbon's dark sheen, a sign of life
or a symptom
of pushing light off, back, off, back off

towards the sun which isn't.

I light the yahrzeit candle, read by its light
fudge the prayer, smear it with my memory palm
clumsy and intent like a toddler.
Irreverent, I blow it out, go to the terrace
and sit dazed all morning in the walled garden
watching jackdaws levitate
and the sky warm and churn.
I feel

my face

go slack

my forehead

tighten

over a headache's swell. A tide, arrive, arrive.

Whose hurt. Mine / Not mine.

Mine / Not mine –

a metronomic drone, a chant I've known
since I was too young to understand but not too young to feel
the ache of this paired schism.

⁂

The city wakes and loudens, gathers clanging sounds.

The ache in my brain
is the sleepless departed
the insomnia of ethics
acid signals etching paths
from neuron
to neuron

— eyes to hands to womb —

escape routes

through a denuded forest

escape routes

that lead

back to the murderer —

the murdered
the cyclic scent of soil
its clutch
its stain
its carbon with all colors — dirt tunnels for the ants — What

is a life. What are humans like.
I scour the city for hidden names. For paved-over graves. I walk in the hot sun to the top of a hill, walk down.
The people of this town stroll in families and couples.
They hold each other's elbows, gently steer
each other where they want to go.

I sweat stain my shirt, return again alone
to the garden where the iron drain gleams.

Buildings sit flush against the sidewalk here, no front yards.
Instead, courtyard gardens hold space hidden.

⁂

Sensations are bones, emotions are muscles, information is skin. A place is a practice. A place is a feeling —

In my walled garden
the jackdaw rots
below the cat's perch.
Nightjars fly south, svelte undersides white
against the now-dark sky.
Faint warmth and soft gold flame of the candle, lit again.

Rosalie lived
in this town

in a stately pink house. She once walked
through the arched dark to the balcony
to watch the bustling street
with a cup of golden tea
her hands sore and paled by starch from sewing shirts.

She pauses for a moment
to listen to the footsteps
of her neighbors
who she trusts –
her neighbors' trusted feet
smooth the trusted cobblestones
and the chatter
of her neighbors' trusted voices
in the shared and trusted city square.

⁂

– some ballast for this lifestorm?

dead / living / loves –

no, they sigh, we too
are molecular successions only

brief living mirrors –
dark mirrors, light mirrors – in which the prophets saw –

⁂

pre-storm
geometric

broken Kaddish

again

I walk

phonemes forgotten
click clack photograph
footfall footfall
orphaned fine-tuned footfall
forget forgot forged identity
cards cart of bones
sternums fibulas
stone-jolted jackdaws
roused to orphaned flight
sacrums occipital orbs orbit
femurs forget
          footfall footfall
Yitgadal v'yitkadash
sh'mei same shame
fall foot orphan
organize organs
a pile for the vultures
for the eyes
the spectacles
          foot found
toe bones
pursed mirror
mercury
what heat what
                    water wants
          to forget
footfall

footfell
          across Birkenau
the heat

⁂

under that same dark arch
trains came
trains went
symmetrical gash

precision terrifies

it's not the evil that's unique

it's the perfection

deterministic

banal

bureaucratic rigor
of my heart my pulse

my life, a long retort

a rewilding

of this precise
sum

this superlative control

now thunder
now rain

⁂

Block 25

no magnet no north
no stacked stone walls
no fields between those walls turning steadily to forests
no forests no phloem no shedding of leaves
no leaves no leaving
no clouds no hollow-boned passerines
no passage
no currency
          no memory
no language
          no memory
no family
no cattle cars no wires no black rifle butts
          no blue gas
no suffocation
no siberian winters no full moons no junes
no austere citizens looking askance
          no thickening plot
                    no thinning ice
no apocalypse the uncovering has been and is

the brain washed clean

no time no clock no calendar no wheel

no brakes no harrowed field

forgetting is what humans do
in order to make stories :

⁂

it's a beautiful day when i visit
mounds of ebullient clouds
swooping swifts, black lilts of predatory elegance
in soft warm air —   empty   entropy

overgrown   plot between   identical

buildings
made of identical bricks

the plot in the block
made of identical identities

identities identified indented wall where the executions took
lacerated wall where the blue gas set

its suffocated supplicants in mounds like bright clouds
dark squares where they piled

where they were kept underground
where they were raped and shaven

where they were stripped denuded sterilized
the weedy plot blooms

about to be mown
down

they told me when i was a child
that punishment was survival
what a thing to tell a child
i believed them
now i know why

gear fangled anguish

why the living
hurt more than it was worth

to the living
to their kin

⁂

where to look and how
straight in the eyes
sideways, at the angle of the jaw

glance, glare, stare, blink
wink, interstitial inward

breaking the outside world
dark in
dark heartbeat heartbeat blood borne brain
blood through pinky toe and elbow

through breast, nipple, mouth, lips
blood through bone, occiput, knee

root weeds water
dark

⁂

Water falls from the sky here

This place I call home
A short lull in diaspora

Water falls in tiny spheres, drips down stalks
of plants' flaring forms
White tea roses plump with petals
Sage and heuchera, fireweed and black rock
Blooms of the maple
gone to samara
soon to spin
and drop
find ground on which to die or grow
both an unfurling

to furl
to fold
to hold
insensate pain
dead nub of
having preferred to have died
of seeking to shrug off
the chronic condition of life
I swill this bitterest medicine
feel it quell the squall somehow

They wanted me to live
prayersharp

a tool
force to form

I'm being breathed
touched back
by the unmown plot
its bees
its iridescent flies
its gnats, spiders, maggots
its swifts in the warm and watery blue
I'm not alone
not mechanized

Even as the studied maintenance
of borders, binds, blinds
is still principal
in our forms

⁂

Waveform of ribs
          sine wave like
the shape of light or sound
          bring it all the way down
and it's always the same : the mesh of all us
          warp weft

gravetree

          lightning storm
thunder over Krakow
          rain trapped in the empty square

a nowhere where
          I slept
          split

          life
the earth, its actuality
          is
us, its witnesses
          forces / forms
the crimson poppies

    by the freeway on the dawn drive to Auschwitz
the stork pacing measured steps through the poppies' swamp
    the swamp exhaling warm wet breath
between the freeway and the little town with its church spire so white
    against the sky's dark heft, set to storm –
Then this backyard garden. Fireweed poised to bloom.
    Nothing is forgotten, only subsumed.

⁂

When I think about furling Rosalie's story, I realize the thread I am trying to spool and hand back to her is split, broken into at least two strands: hers and my own.

Then there is my mother, whose version of Rosalie's story I inherited, too, a version that differs starkly from mine or Rosalie's.

And sometimes, when I'm thinking about Rosalie, I'm thinking about her as an individual, but sometimes I'm thinking about her as a metonym for the Holocaust in my family, and for the ongoing aftershock of individual and collective trauma, violence, and displacement that arose from that nexus of horrors.

And sometimes Rosalie stands in for the Holocaust as a whole. Like the man who would eat the snake, making it part of his body, my family's story is one tiny part of the body of this much larger story, just as this much larger story is part of many individual bodies, including my own.

A frayed thread.

And while the Nazis' approach to genocide was unique because of its thorough enmeshment with capitalism's fundamentalist efficiency, genocide is not. The Holocaust, contrary to dominant Jewish rhetoric, is not exceptional. It's a part of a widespread, embedded system of thinking still very alive today.

Naomi Klein: "[The Holocaust is] a story about a logic, *the* logic that has been ravaging our world for so very long. [...] A people, just like a person, can be victim and victimizer at the same time; they can be both traumatized and traumatizer. So much of modern history is a story of pools of trauma being spatially moved around the globe like chess pieces made of human misery, with yesterday's victims enlisted as today's occupying army."

The harm is everywhere, in us all.

Deep in bodies throughout the world and in the body of the world, the horror holds.

The thread is a wild cloud, a stuck storm.

⁂

How to furl a shredded thread.

How to furl the subtle body of the cataclysm.

How to furl an aching cancer in the core of consciousness.

How to furl an abyssal chimera.

How to furl an ongoing energetic ruin.

How to furl the presence of absence.

How to furl rupture as agency.

How to furl violence that lives on and on and on deep within the invisible.

How to furl silence.

How to furl spite.

How to furl bereftness of meaning made heritable.

How to furl the immortal devil in us all.

⁂

When Einstein published his theories, many greeted them with confusion. Confusion is uncomfortable. Most people tend to resent it and to see it as a threat, a problem to be fixed. Confusion about Einstein's theories quickly gave way to resentment, with dismissal following close on resentment's heels, all powered by the cheap and ever-available fuel of bigotry: Einstein's science was Jewish science, and *Jewish* science was a plot. The Jewish scientists would confuse everyone, upset the natural order of the folk, destabilizing the world so they could subsequently control it.

Einstein's Kabbalistic magic concocted a universe in which it was impossible to say with certainty where you were or what time it was. You could only describe space or time in relation to something else, and that something else could only be described by its spatial or temporal coordinates in relation to you. Clearly, this was nefarious lunacy, a trick of those secretive, powerful Jews—that familiar, durable script.

In contrast, the Nazi worldview was one of absolute, objective truths, a world made of clear and impermeable edges, firm boundary lines. These truths were embodied and understood by a master race whose members exemplified the ideal (truest) human form. There was one true religion and one true language, with cultural forms that were the best (truest) cultural forms because they celebrated these (truest) truths. The comfort of this absolute certainty is undeniable in the face of an increasingly confusing, increasingly unbearable world.

⁂

Hannah Arendt: “In an ever-changing, incomprehensible world the masses had reached the point where they would, at the same time, believe everything and nothing, think that everything was possible and nothing was true.”

Paola Antonetta: “So much of the universe consists of forces that can’t be found.”

Conspiracy theories distract us from the unbearable nothingness at the center of life, at the center of ourselves. They allow us to look the other way.

⁂

Job 26: “Dead things are formed hollow beneath the water. [...] He stretches out the mystery over the empty place / he stretches out the mystery over chaos. He suspends the earth on nothing.”

⁂

Conspiracy theories work like MSG, making everything more palatable in an unspecified way. The tasty molecular logic may not be salutary, but it works—things suddenly taste good, make sense. Part of the power of a successful conspiracy theory is its endless versatility. Its “truth” is safely nonspecific, allowing it to be satisfyingly all-purpose. Its vagueness, the skeleton key to its resilient success. It’s fit to be applied to any potential scenario despite the world’s vicissitudes.

Hannah Arendt: “The opposite of the beautiful is not the ugly but the useful, the good for.”

⁂

Care is infinitely messier and harder than a calcified belief system which obviates the need to care.

⁂

How might we care? How to not be history’s accomplice? How to, in the words of Simone Weil, “never react to an evil in such a way as to augment it”?

⁂

Language is a body that has recesses, pits of muscle memory where, like any body, it can’t help but recall.

I try to extract the mute glimmers; to give them a new, spacious body through which to speak.

A loose grouping of dead conflagrations, reverberating light.

These stars will not constellate, will not cohere into a symbol for myth—no ladles or lions, no aphoristic orbits. At most, these lights will offer an asterism, a clutch of poetic self-contradictions, a vague but lit cluster against which—

⁂

An unreadable confusion of light and dark, all knife-sharp, lullabied and ransacked, cradled and jettisoned, bolstered and eroded, buoyed and drowned.

A torqued magnet, my edges facing each other, facing off: attract, resist, attract, resist—

⁂

In the wilderness where I'd met the man and the snake, the desert rocks around me were orange, brown, and pink—ossified skin, compressed by time and light. It was sunset but I was restless so I parked and hiked a few fast miles to the remains of ancient homes. Built of rough rectangles of chipped, ruddy stone stacked against the caves, the bygone dwellings perch atop the cliffs, overlooking rolling juniper valleys. All the homes are oriented towards one large, deep blue, triangle-shaped hill over which the sun was rapidly setting, a blazing orange circle against the peak's angular blue.

The dwellings, the mountain, the sunset, the hill, my body, the shifting colors, the petroleum fueling my truck: transience and permanence—though I just sat a long time not wanting to write that last word—because what is permanent? *Ein sof*, perhaps, and perhaps the dark light of horror that continues to move without limit or scope.

The earth erodes, preserves some vague concavities. The earth, you and I, are the force of nothingness amplified to form. Absence as presence.

Whatever truth finds life is fast—as in fleeting, as in indelible.

BIBLIOGRAPHY

Akómoláfé, Báyò. "When You Meet the Monster, Anoint Its Feet." *Emergence Magazine*, October 16, 2018. https://emergencemagazine.org/story/when-you-meet-the-monster.

Antonetta, Susanne Paola. *The Terrible Unlikelihood of Our Being Here*. Columbus: Mad Creek Books, 2021.

Arendt, Hannah. *Lectures on Kant's Political Philosophy*. Edited by Ronald Beiner. Chicago: The University Of Chicago Press, 1992.

—. *The Origins of Totalitarianism*. New York: Penguin Classics, 2017.

Benjamin, Walter. *Illuminations*. Translated by Harry Zorn and edited by Hannah Arendt. London: The Bodley Head, 2015.

Bronner, Stephen Eric. *A Rumor about the Jews: Reflections on Antisemitism and the Protocols of the Learned Elders of Zion*. New York: St. Martin's Press, 2000.

Cha, Theresa Hak Kyung. *Dictée*. Berkeley: University of California Press, 2001.

Cheng, Jennifer S. "Dear Blank Space: A Literacy Narrative." *Literary Hub*, December 6, 2022. https://lithub.com/dear-blank-space-a-literary-narrative/.

"The Covenant of the Islamic Resistance Movement: 18 August 1988." Yale Law School. Accessed October 2024. https://avalon.law.yale.edu/20th_century/hamas.asp.

Delbo, Charlotte. *Auschwitz and After*. New Haven: Yale University Press, 1995.

Deresiewicz, William. "Birthrights." *Liberties*, February 5, 2022. https://libertiesjournal.com/articles/birthrights.

Derrida, Jacques. *Specters of Marx: The State of the Debt, the Work of Mourning, and the New International*. Translated by Peggy Kamuf. London: Routledge, 1994.

Eisner, Will. *The Plot: The Secret Story of the Protocols of the Elders of Zion*. New York: W. W. Norton & Company, 2006.

Ekrem, Erica. "Transcript: Donna Haraway on Staying with the Trouble [Encore] / 269." *For the Wild*, January 19, 2022. https://forthewild.world/podcast-transcripts/donna-haraway-on-staying-with-the-trouble-encore-269.

Hejinian, Lyn. *The Language of Inquiry*. Berkeley: University of California Press, 2000.

Herman, Judith. *Trauma and Recovery: The Aftermath of Violence—from Domestic Abuse to Political Terror*. New York: Basic Books, 1992.

Hirsch, Marianne. *The Generation of Postmemory: Writing and Visual Culture after the Holocaust*. New York: Columbia University Press, 2012.

Jacon Ayres Pinto, Danielle, and Cecília Maieron Pereira. "The Concept of Power in Hannah Arendt and Michel Foucault: A Comparative Analysis." *Brazilian Journal of International Relations* 6, no. 2 (September 2017): 344–59. https://doi.org/10.36311/2237-7743.2017.v6n2.07.p344.

Jamison, Peter, and Valerie Strauss. "D.C. Lawmaker Says Recent Snowfall Caused by 'Rothschilds Controlling the Climate.'" *Washington Post*, March 18, 2018. https://www.washingtonpost.com/local/dc-politics/dc-lawmaker-says-recent-snowfall-caused-byrothschilds-controlling-the-climate/2018/03/18/daeb0eae-2ae0-11e8-911f-ca7f68bff0fc_story.html.

Johnson, George. "Quantum Leaps." *The New York Times*, August 3, 2012. https://www.nytimes.com/2012/08/05/books/review/einsteins-jewish-science-by-steven-gimbel.html.

Jung, C. G. *Memories, Dreams, Reflections*. Edited by Aniela Jaffé. Translated by Richard Winston and Clara Winston. New York: Vintage Books, 1989.

Klawans, Justin. "82% of Fox News, 97% of OANN, Newsmax Viewers Believe Trump's Stolen Election Claim: Poll." *Newsweek*, November 1, 2021. https://www.newsweek.com/82-fox-news-97-oann-newsmax-viewers-believe-trumps-stolen-election-claim-poll-1644756.

Klein, Naomi. *Doppelganger: A Trip Into the Mirror World*. Toronto: Knopf Canada, 2023.

Koopman, Colin. "The Power Thinker." *Aeon*, March 15, 2017. https://aeon.co/essays/why-foucaults-work-on-power-is-more-important-than-ever.

Kushner, Lawrence. "Kabbalah and Everyday Mysticism." *On Being*, May 15, 2014. https://onbeing.org/programs/lawrence-kushner-kabbalah-and-everyday-mysticism.

Labatut, Benjamín. *When We Cease to Understand the World*. Translated by Adrian Nathan West. New York: New York Review Books, 2021.

Landes, Richard, and Steven T. Katz. *The Paranoid Apocalypse: A Hundred-Year Retrospective on the Protocols of the Elders of Zion*. New York: New York University Press, 2012.

Lévinas, Emmanuel. *Of God Who Comes to Mind*. Palo Alto: Stanford University Press, 1998.

Luban, David. "Hannah Arendt Meets QAnon: Conspiracy, Ideology, and the Collapse of Common Sense." *Georgetown Law Faculty Publications and Other Works* 2384 (May 2021). https://doi.org/10.2139/ssrn.3852241.

Naimon, David. "Between the Covers Victoria Chang Interview." *Tin House*, January 5, 2022. https://tinhouse.com/transcript/between-the-covers-victoria-chang-interview.

Nelson, Maggie. *On Freedom: Four Songs of Care and Constraint*. Minneapolis: Graywolf Press, 2021.

Nixon, Rob. *Slow Violence and the Environmentalism of the Poor*. Cambridge: Harvard University Press, 2011.

Palmer, Ewan. "Nearly Half of QAnon Followers Believe Jews Plotting to Rule the World." *Newsweek*, June 28, 2021. https://www.newsweek.com/qanon-antisemitism-morning-consult-survey-1604752.

Pisano, Nirit Gradwohl. *Granddaughters of the Holocaust: Never Forgetting What They Didn't Experience*. Boston: Academic Studies Press, 2012.

Rich, Adrienne. *On Lies, Secrets, and Silence: Selected Prose 1966 – 1978*. New York: W. W. Norton & Company, 1995.

Russonello, Giovanni. "QAnon Now as Popular in U.S. As Some Major Religions, Poll Suggests." *The New York Times*, May 27, 2021. https://www.nytimes.com/2021/05/27/us/politics/qanon-republicans-trump.html.

Schaeffer, Katherine. "A Look at the Americans Who Believe There Is Some Truth to the Conspiracy Theory That COVID-19 Was Planned." Pew Research Center, July 24, 2020. https://www.pewresearch.org/fact-tank/2020/07/24/a-look-at-the-americans-who-believe-there-is-some-truth-to-the-conspiracy-theory-that-covid-19-was-planned.

Sefaria. "Sefer Etz Chaim 1:2:2." Sefaria Community Translation. Last modified April 2023. https://www.sefaria.org/Sefer_Etz_Chaim.1.2.2?lang=bi.

Shimoda, Brandon. *The Grave on the Wall*. San Francisco: City Lights Publishers, 2019.

Stephens, Bret. "What an Antisemite's Fantasy Says about Jewish Reality." *The New York Times*, January 21, 2022. https://www.nytimes.com/2022/01/21/opinion/texas-synagogue-antisemitism.html.

United States Holocaust Memorial Museum. "Protocols of the Elders of Zion: Key Dates." Holocaust Encyclopedia. Accessed November 2024. https://encyclopedia.ushmm.org/content/en/article/protocols-of-the-elders-of-zion-key-dates.

Van der Kolk, Bessel. *The Body Keeps the Score: Brain, Mind, and Body in the Healing of Trauma*. New York: Penguin Books, 2014.

Weil, Simone. *First and Last Notebooks: Supernatural Knowledge*. Translated by Richard Rees. Eugene: Wipf & Stock Publishers, 2015.

Wolynn, Mark. *It Didn't Start with You: How Inherited Family Trauma Shapes Who We Are and How to End the Cycle*. New York: Penguin Books, 2016.

Yehuda, Rachel. "How Trauma and Resilience Cross Generations." *On Being*, November 9, 2017. https://onbeing.org/programs/rachel-yehuda-how-trauma-and-resilience-cross-generations-nov2017.

Yehuda, Rachel, Nikolaos P. Daskalakis, Linda M. Bierer, Heather N. Bader, Torsten Klengel, Florian Holsboer, and Elisabeth B. Binder. "Holocaust Exposure Induced Intergenerational Effects on FKBP5 Methylation." *Biological Psychiatry* 80, no. 5 (August 2016): 372 – 80. https://doi.org/10.1016/j.biopsych.2015.08.005.

Zapruder, Matthew. Introduction to *The Lice*, by W. S. Merwin. Port Townsend: Copper Canyon Press, 2017.

ACKNOWLEDGMENTS

This book is for my family—past, present, and future. And for Rosalie: I heard you then, I hear you now.

"MINUTES: A Remembrance" could not have been written without my mother, Martha Leb Molnar's book, *To Life*, a remarkable feat of historical reconstruction, combining extensive research with imagination to convey the substance of lives that were abruptly ended without record. It is the story of one person and her family, it is the story of the unique Jewish culture that existed in Transylvania for centuries and is now extinct, and it is the story of global sociopolitical shifts from the late nineteenth century to the present day, illuminating how these global changes alter families and individuals for generations. Thank you, Mom.

Thank you, Jason Francisco, for the ongoing poetic kinship and for your good company with the ghosts.

Thank you, Daniela Fernandez, for your vivid, invincible spirit. Thank you for cocreating our wild ride of aliveness in (of all places) Poland. And thank you for reading and for so deeply receiving *The Lost*, parts of which found a home in this book.

Thank you, friends, for reading versions of this work and offering compassionate, insightful feedback: Casey A. Boyle, Jay Ponteri, Sebastian Merrill, Aaron Hauptman, and Adie B. Steckel.

Thank you, Anne Germanacos, for your myriad forms of generosity, mentorship, and love.

Thank you, Poetry Church, for the laughter, learning, copious coffee, cats, donuts, gardens, and camaraderie.

Thank you, Rabbi Josh Rose, Nina Elder, Anne-Sophie Balzer, Jane Terzibashian, and The Empty Room Collective. Our conversations sustained me and this project more than you might know.

Thank you to the many writers, artists, journalists, scientists, and philosophers whose words appear in this book or informed my research. Your work formed the ecosystem within which this project learned to live.

Thank you, Michael. This book often left me feeling disoriented, adrift in a sad sea. Again and again, you swam to me, offering laughter, language, and new ways to live, see, and feel.

*

Thank you, Ayin. What a team! And special gratitude to Eden for the ecstatic editing and spirited phone calls. You made this book shine.

Thank you to the Western States Center for believing in artists as a crucial part of cultural change. This book and its related projects never would have happened if not for your extensive support.

Thank you to the following residencies and fellowships for providing the gift of time and space to make this book: PLAYA, Ucross, Sou'wester, The Sitka Center for Art & Ecology, Spring Creek Project, and Co/Lab.

This book is funded in part by the Regional Arts & Culture Council. Thank you for the crucial support.

A PARTIAL INDEX OF *PROTOCOLS* COVERS

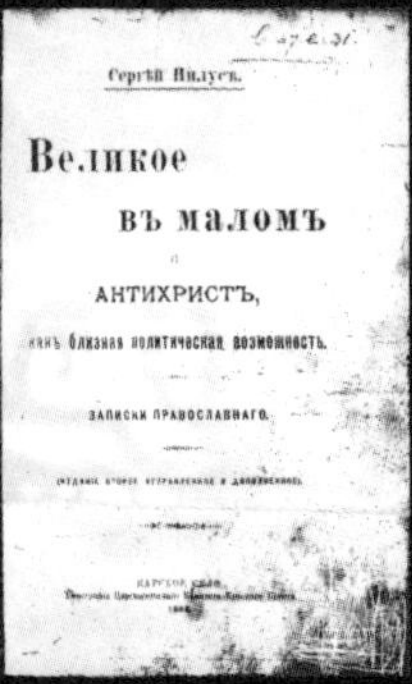

Сергѣй Нилусъ.
Великое
въ маломъ
АНТИХРИСТЪ,
какъ близкая политическая возможность.
ЗАПИСКИ ПРАВОСЛАВНАГО.

RUSSIAN EMPIRE
1903

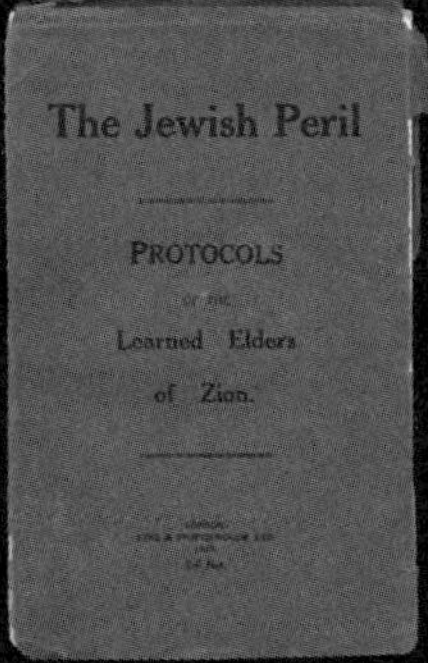

The Jewish Peril
PROTOCOLS
of the
Learned Elders
of Zion.

ENGLAND
1920

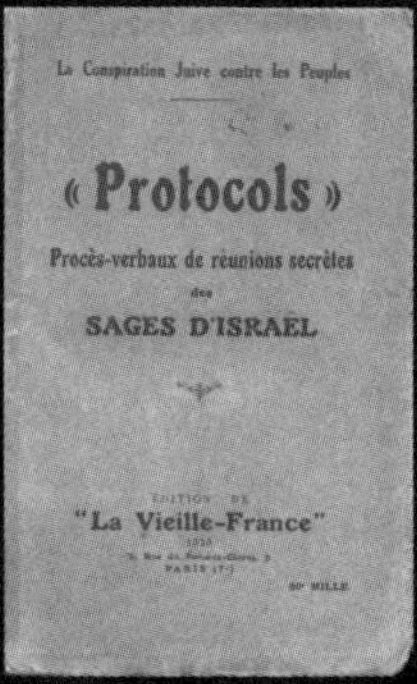

La Conspiration Juive contre les Peuples
« Protocols »
Procès-verbaux de réunions secrètes
des
SAGES D'ISRAEL
"La Vieille-France"

FRANCE
1920

Die
Geheimnisse
der Weisen von Zion

GERMANY
1920

THE PROTOCOLS AND
WORLD REVOLUTION
BOSTON
SMALL, MAYNARD & COMPANY

UNITED STATES
1920

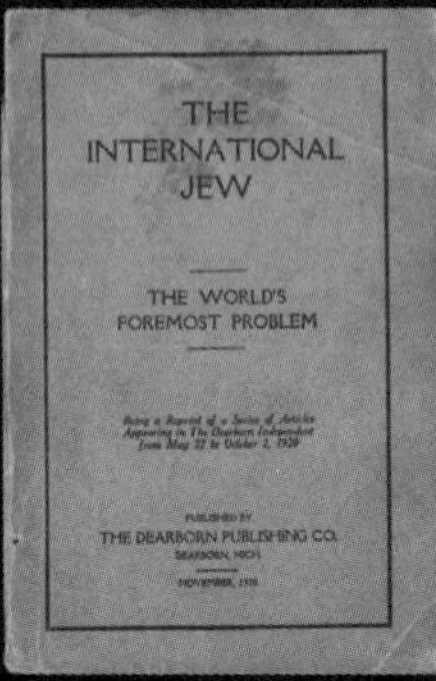

THE
INTERNATIONAL
JEW
THE WORLD'S
FOREMOST PROBLEM
PUBLISHED BY
THE DEARBORN PUBLISHING CO.

UNITED STATES
1920

1930
EL GOBIERNO
MUNDIAL INVISIBLE
O
EL PROGRAMA JUDIO
PARA SUBYUGAR AL
MUNDO

PROTOCOLOS
DE LOS SABIOS DE
SION

Die Protokolle der
Weisen von Zion
und die jüdische
Weltpolitik
von
Alfred Rosenberg

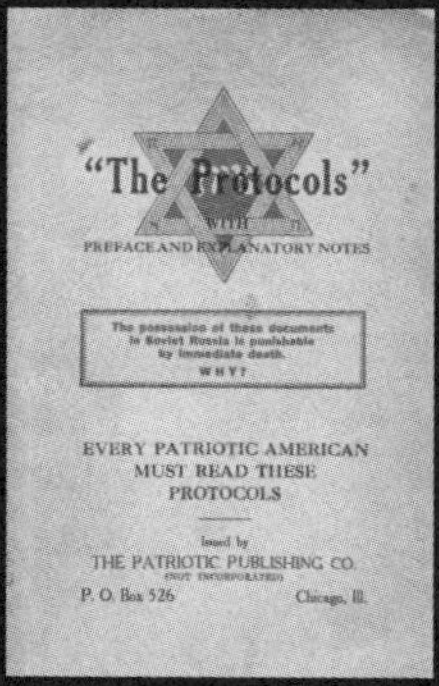
"The Protocols"
WITH
PREFACE AND EXPLANATORY NOTES
The possession of these documents in Soviet Russia is punishable by immediate death. WHY?
EVERY PATRIOTIC AMERICAN MUST READ THESE PROTOCOLS
Issued by
THE PATRIOTIC PUBLISHING CO.
(NOT INCORPORATED)
P. O. Box 526 Chicago, Ill.

UNITED STATES
1934

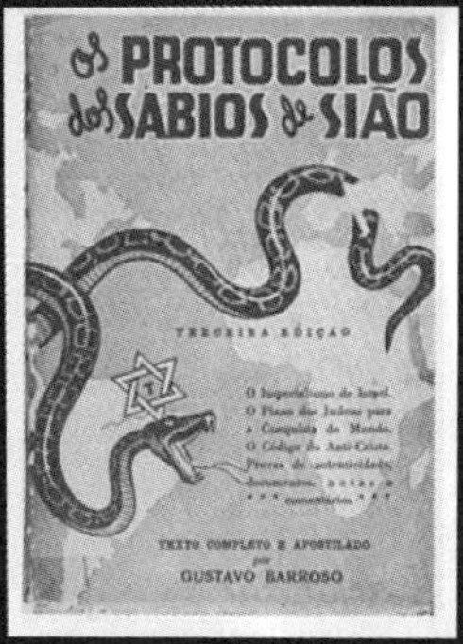
Os PROTOCOLOS dos SABIOS de SIÃO
TERCEIRA EDIÇÃO
O Imperialismo de Israel. O Plano dos Judeus para a Conquista do Mundo. O Código do Anti-Cristo. Provas de autenticidade, documentos, notas e comentarios
TEXTO COMPLETO E APOSTILADO
por
GUSTAVO BARROSO

BRAZIL
1937

JEWISH CONSPIRACY
THE PROTOCOLS OF THE LEARNED ELDERS OF ZION

PAKISTAN
1969

عجاج نويهض
بروتوكولات حكماء صهيون
نصوصها، رموزها، أصولها التلمودية
مجموعة الأجزاء الأربعة

LEBANON
1996

بروتوكولات حكماء صهيون
رجا عبد الحميد عرابي

SYRIA
2005

The Classic on International Zionism
With comments by Henry Ford, Founder of the Ford Motor Company
Protocols of the Learned Elders of Zion
Foreword by Texe Marrs

UNITED STATES
2011

the PROTOCOLS of the LEARNED ELDERS of ZION
sergei nilus

UNITED STATES
2019

THE PROTOCOLS OF THE LEARNED ELDERS OF ZION

UNITED STATES
2021

CLEMENS & BLAIR
PROTOCOLS of the ELDERS of ZION
The Definitive English Edition
Edited and Translated by
THOMAS DALTON, PhD

UNITED STATES
2023

Daniela Naomi Molnar is a poet, artist, and writer who creates with color, water, language, and place. Her debut book, *CHORUS*, won the 2024 Oregon Book Award for Poetry and was selected by Kazim Ali as the winner of Omnidawn Press's 1st/2nd Book Award. Her paintings are created with pigments she makes from plants, bones, stones, rainwater, and glacial melt. Forthcoming books include *Memory of a Larger Mind* (Omnidawn, 2028) and *Light / Remains* (Bored Wolves Press, 2026). Her book-length poem "Memory of a Larger Mind" accompanies photographs by Julian Stettler in *The Glacier Is a Being* (Sturm & Drang, 2023). Her work is anthologized in the forthcoming second volume of *The Ecopoetry Anthology* and in *Breaking the Glass: A Contemporary Jewish Poetry Anthology* from the *Laurel Review*. Molnar lives in Portland, Oregon and in the high deserts of the North American West. *www.danielamolnar.com* / Instagram: *@daniela_naomi_molnar*

Ayin Press is an independent publishing house rooted in Jewish culture and emanating outward.

Both online and in print, we seek to celebrate artists and thinkers at the margins and explore the growing edges of collective consciousness through a diverse range of mediums and genres.

Ayin was founded on a deep belief in the power of culture and creativity to heal, transform, and uplift the world we share and build together. We are committed to amplifying a polyphony of voices from within and beyond the Jewish world.

For more information about our current or upcoming projects and titles, reach out to us at *info@ayinpress.org*. To make a tax-deductible contribution to our work, visit our website at *www.ayinpress.org/donate*.

(power)

(power)

(power)